Elsy Feels Better

by Ali Freer

illustrated by Alette Straathof

Elsy the Elephant looked into a pool of water. *Drip!* A big tear fell in with a splash.

Elsy didn't like feeling glum. She walked off wearily to talk to Granny Greta.

"It's not fun being sad!" said Elsy.
"Can I be happy all the time?"

"If there *is* one animal in the whole forest who is always happy," Granny said. "Then maybe you *can* always be happy!"

Elsy went off and found Herby.

"Are you ever sad?" Elsy asked.

"Oh, yes," said Herby. "Yesterday, I lost my best hat."

Elsy walked on. She found Charly.

"Charly, are you ever sad?" she asked.

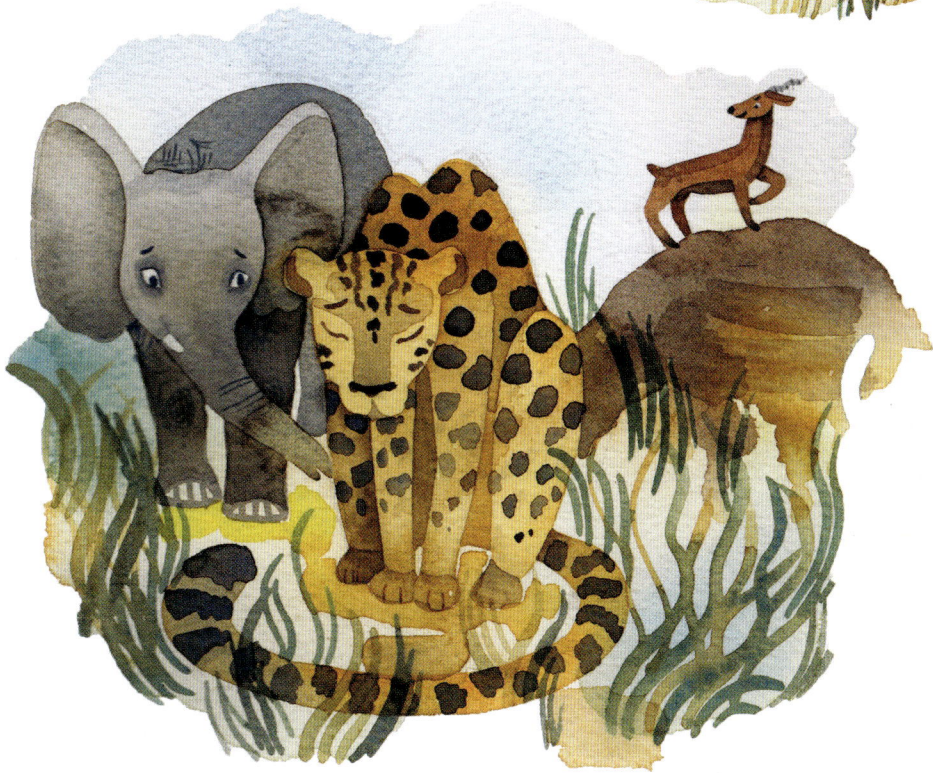

"Oh, yes!" said Charly, looking at his paws. "Yesterday, Gabby beat me in a race!"

Elsy walked on. She saw Milly, who was always chirpy.

"Milly, you are never sad, are you?" she asked.

"It's true, I am always happy!" said Milly.

"Hurray!" said Elsy.

Just then, a mango fell on Milly's arm.
Milly started to sob, loudly.

Ouch!

"Oh dear!" said Elsy.

She stayed until Milly felt better.

Then Elsy went off to think. How could she make everyone happy?

Suddenly, she had a plan! She would throw a party!

Milly and Charly put up balloons.
Herby made cakes.

As Elsy made the invites, she felt restful and content.

Everyone said a party would be fun!
Elsy felt lucky to have such terrific pals.

Yes!

Hurray!

Terrific!

The animals all had a fantastic time. Granny Greta sat in the corner enjoying the fun.

"So, who in the whole forest is never sad?" Granny asked Elsy.

"No one," said Elsy. "Everyone is sad sometimes and that's okay."

"With a little help, we can feel better in no time!" said Elsy.

As Elsy looked around, she felt full of joy!

Thanks for the invite!

Thanks for your help!

Want a race?

Have you seen my hat?

23

Look Back

Encourage the child to use the pictures to retell the story.
Ask them to think about what made Elsy feel better.